DAILY THOUGHTS COLLECTIONS

VOLUME I

DAILY THOUGHTS COLLECTIONS

VOLUME I

Mark Fritz

Procedor Publications
London, England

First Edition
Paperback ISBN: 9781548392079

CONTENTS

COLLECTIONS

COLLECTION 1

**Thoughts on Living
a Fulfilling Life**

FEEL GOOD OR DO GOOD?

Motivational books make you feel good,
but the goal is to DO good.

Ponder this:

*Go beyond reading motivational books to feel good...
use the ideas, insights and recommendations to take
more action and create the life you truly want.*

INSIDE REDUCES OUTSIDE PRESSURE

Life is far easier when you discipline yourself to act before others force you to.

Ponder this:

Life actually becomes easier when you discipline yourself to do what you know is necessary before others force you to do it.

YOUR STRUGGLES GIVE YOU STRENGTH

You are always a stronger person on the other side of the struggles you face.

Ponder this:

Learn to look beyond the struggles you face today to the benefit they have in making you a stronger person who can take on even bigger challenges.

FILL YOUR SHOES

A great goal is living the type of life that inspires others to fill your shoes.

Ponder this:

The way you live your life can become a model for others – so live your life in ways that inspire others to follow your example.

WHY NOT BE DIFFERENT?

Your uniqueness makes you different. Live your life to make a bigger difference to others.

Ponder this:

You have unique abilities that others don't have; use your uniqueness to make a bigger difference in the world around you.

ACTION CREATES THE BEST FEELING

Isn't it true that the happiest people
are always taking action?

Ponder this:

*You never see a happy person just sitting around all the
time. They are taking action, living life to its fullest, and
enjoying every minute of it too.*

SERIOUS AND FUN

You should be serious in choosing your passion, but have fun in living it.

Ponder this:

A passion's strength is in making a difference to others. Choose a passion that makes a big difference and provides you the most fun in making it happen.

DEFINED BY WHO YOU ARE

Happy people define themselves by who they are rather than the status they have achieved.

Ponder this:

Status is an outcome of achievement, but not a way of life. Define yourself by the person you are versus the status you attain.

DECISIONS ALIGNED WITH VALUES

People living with high stress often make decisions inconsistent with their values.

Ponder this:

In times of stress, you need to remind yourself of your values. This prevents stress from driving your behaviors outside the boundaries of your values.

LEAVE BEFORE YOU GO

Many people try to focus on the future without letting go of the past.

Ponder this:

Learn from the past, then let it go. If not, the past may consume your thoughts and reduce your focus on the future.

TIME OR ATTENTION

In building relationships, it's not the percent of time, but the percent of attention.

Ponder this:

Attention, not time, is what keeps your relationships with others strong. Focus on being 100 percent present when you are with others.

THANK YOU POWER

People take so much for granted...
differentiate yourself by saying THANK YOU.

Ponder this:

*Say thank you to others in ways that they appreciate most.
The goal is making others feel better in their own
unique way.*

TAKE YOURSELF BEYOND YOUR PAST

You prevent yourself from living in the past by focusing on the future you want.

Ponder this:

You become what you think about, so always focus your thoughts on your future goals and the person you need to become to achieve them faster.

FURTHER THAN YESTERDAY

Life is a journey and success is going to a new place by learning every day.

Ponder this:

Your success comes faster when you decide to invest time to learn something new each day, and find a way to apply the lesson that week too.

CLARITY OF PURPOSE

Your clarity of purpose drives your life's direction and determines whether you enjoy the trip.

Ponder this:

Invest time to stay clear on your purpose, as the direction of your life helps you to see more ways to enjoy the trip to achieve that purpose.

STAY IN THE MOMENT

People who get things done are able to give a 100% focus to what they do.

Ponder this:

Give 100% to what you are doing right now.
You will do a better job at it and you will complete if faster.
Remember, you cannot do two things at once.

LIVE YOUR BELIEFS

The happiest people are those who live their beliefs. Being "true to you" is key.

Ponder this:

You are happy when you live within your beliefs, and are constantly evaluating your beliefs to make sure they are consistent with your dreams.

THINK AND FEEL WHO YOU ARE

Who you think and feel you are is the driver of who you will become.

Ponder this:

Competence is a foundation. It is really your own thoughts and feelings about your competence that enable you to achieve what you want in life.

PEOPLE WHO GIVE YOU ENERGY

Life is much easier when you surround yourself with people who give you energy.

Ponder this:

Do a little review of your network, friends and family and focus more of your time with the people that give you energy when you are around them.

GOODBYE IS ALSO HELLO

As the saying goes, when one door closes...
another one opens.

Ponder this:

Not every opportunity will work out for you, but keep the belief that there will always be more opportunities coming along. Be prepared for them.

YOU CAN'T GIVE WHAT YOU DON'T HAVE

Make the decision to be happy. You can't give what you don't have yourself.

Ponder this:

People who are happy make the decision to be happy. Decide to be happy and you will naturally influence others around you to feel the same way.

IMAGINE YOURSELF LIVING IT

Build your growth by imagining the life you want and boosting the passion to get it.

Ponder this:

When you build the WHY for your life and focus on it, it will also grow the passion within you to take more action on it every day.

LOSE IT TO GAIN IT

Decide to give up (lose) in order to make time available for what you want to win.

Ponder this:

As you rise in any organization, you grow faster by identifying what you need to give up in order to invest your time in what will grow you faster.

GAP TO POTENTIAL?

Know your potential and always have a more fulfilling life achieving it.

Ponder this:

Believing in your potential will drive you to become the person who is capable of achieving it... making your life far more fulfilling.

SEE YOURSELF MAKING A DIFFERENCE

Invest time to define your difference and life becomes much more meaningful.

Ponder this:

Think through what unique abilities enable you to do what others can't, then focus on using them more often to make a bigger difference.

CHANGE WHAT HAPPENS IN ME

Happiness is not driven by what change happens in others, but the change in you.

Ponder this:

You are the driver of your own happiness, not others. Look within yourself each day to be happy versus expecting others to provide it for you.

LET GO OF MISTAKES QUICKLY

Learn from your mistakes. Consider them problems only if you keep repeating them.

Ponder this:

Mistakes are proof that you are taking action. Learn from your mistakes, then let them go.

ASKING FOR HELP IS A SIGN OF STRENGTH

Not asking for help is a weakness.
It limits the pace of your development.

Ponder this:

*Trying to do everything without help slows
your own development. It's best to think
WHO (could help) before HOW.*

BALANCE HAS A TIMEFRAME

Balance is achieved more over a month than it is over a week.

Ponder this:

People want balance and want it now.
You gain balance over time, so focus on activities
that promote balance throughout the month.

START FROM WHERE YOU WANT TO BE

Where you want to be creates the emotional power to drive you there.

Ponder this:

You cannot build the life you want without having a clear picture of what it is. Invest the time to design the life you want in as much detail as you can.

BE PRESENT IN THE MOMENT

Stay present and give 100% of your attention to the current moment.

Ponder this:

Being present in the moment makes you productive in your individual tasks and more influential in your conversations with others.

HOLD OR SHARE POWER

You will never be able to take a relaxing holiday if you are not able to share power.

Ponder this:

You will have more power the more you share, as power is multiplied through your people faster than anything you could ever do by yourself.

LIVE WITHIN YOUR SWEET SPOT

People are the happiest living at the intersection of their strengths and passions.

Ponder this:

When you are using your strengths within your passion, you often gain energy by working hard. Your sweet spot has the power to create energy.

SEE EVERYONE AS IMPORTANT

When you see everyone as important, you see the best in everyone too.

Ponder this:

Your influence with others increases when you see everyone as important. With time, you will see the best in them, and in return, get the best from them.

GIVES MEANING IN LIFE

Passion is necessary in order to bring meaning to what you do every day.

Ponder this:

Work within your passion each day, and each day will have more meaning for you. Your passion is always your source for more energy.

IN MOMENTS OF OPPORTUNITY

The best moments in life are when opportunities come your way.

Ponder this:

Opportunities are coming to you all the time, so be prepared for them. You will then see more of them, and take advantage of them more often too.

APPOINTMENT WITH YOUR FAMILY

Schedule appointments with your family as you do with your job.

Ponder this:

You can live a more productive and fulfilled life by putting your most important appointments (both work and personal) into your schedule first.

BEING MORE POWERFUL THAN HAVING

Who you are is more fulfilling than
what you have. Being trumps having.

Ponder this:

Don't worry about what you have;
reflect about what you can become.
The more you become the more you have.

BALANCE COMPETING PRIORITIES

There are always different priorities to balance. Don't waste time choosing yours.

Ponder this:

Life is all about balancing priorities...so if you don't balance them first, others will balance them for you... and not to your advantage.

FREEDOM IS NEVER FREE

Freedom is never free...it is earned by taking personal responsibility for everything you do.

Ponder this:

You earn your freedom every day. The personal responsibility you bring to everything you do earns you more freedom of choice in how you live your life.

BALANCE OF IN AND OUT

Life is about balancing what is both inside and outside your comfort zone.

Ponder this:

You will grow faster when you live each day outside your comfort zone. In this way you are constantly expanding your comfort zone to achieve more.

GET HELP PAST THE ADVERSITY

Your friends are the people who help you get past the adversity you encounter.

Ponder this:

Friends are naturally there during the good times. However, the full value of your friends is when they are there to help you through adversity.

GRATITUDE GENERATES GENEROSITY

The more gratitude you feel, the more generously you give your time to others.

Ponder this:

Stop and be grateful for what you have in your life, and you will become a better leader as you feel more generosity towards others.

IS IT SUSTAINABLE?

If your pace is not sustainable, you need to improve the way you are working.

Ponder this:

People who can maintain a high pace in their work are constantly looking for ways to improve the way they work. Focus on improving every day.

WHEN YOU HAVE HELP

When you can surround yourself with great people, no problem is too big.

Ponder this:

You multiply your own abilities with the abilities of the people you surround yourself with, and suddenly there is no problem you cannot solve together.

PREPARED TO BE RELAXED

Do your preparation and you will be more relaxed within the moment.

Ponder this:

Being prepared helps you feel more confident and relaxed in the moment and that you can handle anything that comes along.

RELAXATION IS TRAINABLE

Everyone can relax more, but as with anything, it is about creating a habit.

Ponder this:

Try different ways to relax and see what works best. Once you have found it, then discipline yourself to keep doing it until it becomes a habit.

INVEST IN MORE PERSONAL LIFE

You remember events in your personal life far more than events in your work life.

Ponder this:

You can keep a great perspective by scheduling both your important personal and work commitments.

BELIEFS DETERMINE YOUR HAPPINESS

Beliefs, not experiences, are what determine your happiness every day.

Ponder this:

Your experiences each day can be both good and bad, but when you control your beliefs about them, you have control over your happiness too.

YOU NEVER RETIRE FROM LIFE

You never retire from life...only change your focus to the opportunities available.

Ponder this:

As you go through life, your opportunities change and you will need to change your focus at times to take advantage of those opportunities.

IT WASN'T WORTH IT

When you work instead of attending a family event, it wasn't really worth it.

Ponder this:

You will remember your experiences with others more than your own. Don't miss your most important family experiences...plan to attend them.

SELF-FULFILLING PROPHECY

If you expect the worst to happen, you often find what makes it happen too.

Ponder this:

Keep your expectations positive and you will see more positive circumstances and results as well. There's an old saying: you get what you expect.

COLLECTION 2

Thoughts on Managing Your Time

STAY TRUE TO YOUR PURPOSE

You always get your energy recharged when you stay true to your purpose.

Ponder this:

There is something about a purpose that gives you strength whenever you think about it or take action. Prioritize your purpose each day.

TIME IS NOT THE SAME FOR EVERYONE

People who put a high value on time usually get more money for their time.

Ponder this:

Don't sell yourself short. Put a high value on your time, have the courage to demand that value from others. You will find that they will soon respect it.

GIVE YOURSELF THE TIME

People with less stress do upfront planning about how they use their time.

Ponder this:

Invest more time to think ahead and plan your day or week. Planning helps you to use your time in more productive ways and to achieve more too.

POWER IN WHAT YOU IGNORE

What you ignore provides you the time to focus on the important and achieve it.

Ponder this:

Distractions will always come. Choosing to ignore some of them will give you more time to focus on those connected to your goals.

TIME BOX THE UGLY

Set a time limit for things you don't like doing and challenge yourself to beat it.

Ponder this:

You can do the things you like doing more often when you give yourself less time to do the things you don't enjoy. Use your creativity to do them in less time.

ACTIVITY CAN BE YOUR ENEMY

Just being busy is really your enemy. Focus on progress and achievement.

Ponder this:

Activity can be your enemy. Getting things done doesn't always means something is being achieved. Focus on progress and achievement.

NEVER YOUR NUMBER ONE PROBLEM

The problem of time is just simply a symptom of lacking a clear focus.

Ponder this:

Everyone has the same of amount of time, so using it as an excuse is pointless. Discipline yourself to keep a clear focus and you will use your time more effectively.

APPEARS MORE DIFFICULT, BUT ISN'T

If you don't invest time to understand something, it often appears more difficult.

Ponder this:

What you don't understand always looks more difficult at first. Invest the time to understand, and then put your focus on the action you can take.

CREATE YOUR OWN MEANING

To keep motivated, we have to find our own meaning in what we are asked to do.

Ponder this:

Don't always wait for others to give you the meaning. Your control over your life begins when you find your own meaning before others give it to you.

APPRECIATE TIME

Value the time of others, and others will begin to value your time as well.

Ponder this:

The more you appreciate your own time, the more others will appreciate your time too. If they don't see you waste theirs, then they won't waste yours either.

TIME AND ATTENTION

In relationships, it's not the amount of time,
but amount of attention you give others.

Ponder this:

Give others your full attention when you are with them.
They will feel more valued, and leave feeling that time
with you is very valuable to them too.

TIME FOR THE IMPORTANT

For the successful, time for the important
always goes into the calendar FIRST.

Ponder this:

*Schedule the important into your day first, and then
get creative about fitting all the rest in. Always think
about the important first.*

AIM IS A GREAT WAY TO FOCUS

Having a target is great for your focus.
It's about what gets you there faster.

Ponder this:

It's difficult to hit a target you do not have. Get clear and stay clear on your target, and you will see more ways to take action to achieve it.

COMPETE WITH THE IMPORTANT

You move forward faster by forcing the urgent to compete with the important.

Ponder this:

The urgent should have some competition. Keep your focus and never let the urgent but unimportant steal time and action away from the important.

PAY THE PRICE EARLY

Pay the price early. Do what is necessary now to deliver better value later on.

Ponder this:

When you do what is necessary early on, you often build a foundation for better results in the future.

PREPARED TO SAY NO MORE OFTEN

With a clear focus, you are much better prepared to say NO, and keep that focus.

Ponder this:

Unfocused people tend to say yes far too often. Invest time to keep your focus strong, and have the courage to say NO more often to others.

BALANCE OF URGENCY AND PATIENCE

There are times when having a little
patience pays off in the long run.

Ponder this:

*When an important relationship requires you
to be a little more patient than you would like to be,
make time to preserve it.*

CLOCK NEVER STOPS RUNNING

Time versus money is the scarcest resource you have, so treat it appropriately.

Ponder this:

When time is lost, it's gone, but money can be regained. Consider your time as your most valuable asset (more than money), and you will enjoy a better life.

DELEGATE TO RAISE YOUR GAME

When you do things better done by others, it's really difficult to raise your game.

Ponder this:

You cannot raise your game unless you have some room to raise it. Delegate more to your people and you will have more room for your own growth.

MARKING TIME = TIME IS UP

Life is a continuous improvement.
When you begin marking time...time is up.

Ponder this:

Focus on looking for and improving something each day.
When you stop improving, you really stop living.
Improving means chasing your potential.

MOST IMPORTANT TIME

The most important time is NOW.
Achievement is accumulated NOWs.

Ponder this:

Achievement is based on progress, and the best way of looking at progress is doing NOW whatever you can to move closer to your goals.

BEST USE OF MY TIME RIGHT NOW?

Ask "What's the best use of my time right now?" to make better choices each day.

Ponder this:

The most important choice is how your time is spent. That time is NOW. Ask yourself, "Is what I am doing now helping me get closer to my goals?"

TREAT TIME AS MONEY

Successful people treat time as money, managing it well... because it really is money.

Ponder this:

Money grabs your attention more than time.
So treat time as money, and be aware of how you invest
your time each day, in order to use it more profitably.

ON THE CRITICAL PATH OF EVERYTHING

Leaders who don't delegate find themselves on the critical path of EVERYTHING.

Ponder this:

Have the courage to delegate more to your people, or you will find yourself in the middle of every decision within the team.

LOSING TRACK OF TIME

If you are working in your passion, you tend to lose track of your time while enjoying it.

Ponder this:

When you haven't noticed the time, you may have been working within your passion. A passion has a way of commanding your full attention and eliminating distractions.

FOCUS TIME FOR YOUR FOCUS

Unless you invest quality time in key focus areas, you can never achieve your goals.

Ponder this:

Successful people invest quality time in their most important priorities. The unsuccessful invest time wherever their attention wanders, often on unimportant matters.

FOCUS IS A COMPETITIVE ADVANTAGE

Everyone gets same amount of time, so create a focus to make the best use of it.

Ponder this:

Focus your time by understanding what's important and schedule it into your day before anything else. If you get distracted, go right back to the important.

CREATE A NO LONGER TO DO LIST

Find the time for what you want to do...
by stopping what you shouldn't be doing.

Ponder this:

It is so difficult to stop what you like doing, but sometimes it is the very thing that is draining time from your truly important goals.

DANGER OF CONVENIENT EXCUSES

You can get results or make excuses...
just not both at the same time.

Ponder this:

Eliminate your excuses and your results will improve by default. Excuses take your eye off achievement, causing you to lose focus and action.

CONFIRM WHAT'S MOST IMPORTANT

You need to invest time in reflection to get clarity about what's most important.

Ponder this:

Unless you reflect regularly, you lose focus. Reflection time has a way of magnifying the important for you.

MATTER OF TIME

Once you have confidence in your ability to make things happen, it's just a matter of time.

Ponder this:

A belief in yourself is something that can add more power to anything you do. With this belief, it is not a matter of if, but of when.

KNOW WHERE IT IS GOING

The most successful people know where their time goes. Do you?

Ponder this:

You might be amazed at the time you waste.
Decide up front where your time will go,
and you will waste less of it.

VALUE YOU PUT ON YOUR TIME

Others will only value your time to the level that YOU value your time.

Ponder this:

How you value your time is based on when you say yes and when you say no. Say yes all the time and others will take advantage of your time.

READY WHEN IT'S YOUR TIME

Successful people prepare and are ready when the opportunities come.

Ponder this:

Being prepared is key to be acting forcefully and quickly when opportunities come. Do you invest in preparation time?

DOWN TIME CREATES BETTER UP TIME

Ideas from our time off drive more achievement in our time on.

Ponder this:

People never say they get the best ideas in the office.
Set aside time for activities where your mind is off work,
and it is amazing the ideas that come in.

CONSTRAINTS DRIVE MORE INNOVATION

Unlimited (or even sufficient) time and money can destroy innovation.

Ponder this:

With finite time and money, do you get more creative about what you do? Constraints can drive your people to more creative solutions.

TIME CAN BE YOUR BIGGEST PROBLEM

Productive people decide how much time to dedicate to a task upfront, and stick to it.

Ponder this:

You become more creative when you set boundaries and stick to them. Time is a great constraint to drive creativity.

TIME TO THINK

You have **never** heard a successful person say "I never have the time to think!"

Ponder this:

Your thoughts drive your actions, so to optimize what you achieve, take the time to think things through. Invest time to think each day.

WHERE DID IT GO?

Only people with a clear focus know where their time goes!

Ponder this:

Unless you have a clear command of your priorities, you will have no clue where your time goes.

POWER OF UNINTERRUPTED TIME

The successful protect their uninterrupted time. Success is born first in thought.

Ponder this:

Your thinking time is when you multiply your power. Block off uninterrupted time each day to think through your important goals to foster more action.

NEVER AN EXCUSE

Lack of time is not an excuse. Everyone gets the same amount! It's a focus problem.

Ponder this:

You can never use time as an excuse. Stop complaining about it and start using it. Keep your focus strong and discipline yourself to achieve it.

OWN SCHEDULE

Delegate to get more control of your time...
Stop micromanaging in the moment.

Ponder this:

Find more ways to delegate jobs to your people and do so in ways that give them more time to do a good job too.

GAIN CLARITY

The time you invest to get CLARITY is an investment in yourself and your future.

Ponder this:

Invest the time your need to get clear and stay clear, and you will find more ways to achieve the future you really want.

PRIORITIZE

Some never focus on the important as they never prioritize the important.

Ponder this:

You cannot focus on something you haven't defined first. So, the first step is to define what's important for you and the reason behind its importance.

MANAGE LIFE OR LIFE MANAGES YOU

Goals help you make the right choices.
Or are you letting your life manage you?

Ponder this:

Without goals, you leave yourself open to let the world manage you. Goals help you move your life in the direction you want to take it.

NOT DOING IT ALL

The best way to achieve it all is not doing it all. Learn to delegate more to your people.

Ponder this:

You cannot achieve success on your own, so fully utilize the talent around you to achieve more success. You can delegate more than you think you can.

FOCUS MANAGEMENT

Everyone has the same amount of time. You cannot manage time, only your focus.

Ponder this:

Time is a commodity, as everyone has the same amount. You turn it into an advantage when you focus your time better than others.

MANAGE TIME IN SMALL SEGMENTS

Think ahead, and manage your time in small segments with specific outcomes.

Ponder this:

Set aside small dedicated blocks of time on specific tasks, and you will make more progress. Dedicated time is what produces results.

THINGS THAT ONLY YOU CAN DO

Focus on what only you can do;
the rest have the potential to be delegated.

Ponder this:

*Make a list of what you and only you can do, and can
never be delegated. It's probably a short list, so everything
else could be delegated with some boundaries.*

MANAGE FOCUS AND ENERGY

Keys to getting more done: stay focused and apply all your energy to that focus.

Ponder this:

Getting more done is easier when you are disciplined to keep your focus, and motivated to take action on that focus whenever you can. Like right now.

IT'S ACHIEVEMENT MANAGEMENT

Effectiveness is not getting more done, it's about achieving more with less effort.

Ponder this:

Think beyond achieving more, but achieving more with less. Constantly look for better ways to use the time you have available each day.

TREAT TIME AS MONEY

Manage a limited resource (Time) and gain an unlimited resource (Money).

Ponder this:

Manage your time effectively and you will find better opportunities to make more money. You can add more value to others when you value your own time first.

COLLECTION 3

**Thoughts on Gaining
a Competitive Edge**

A BETTER DECISION EVERY DAY

Success comes when you make a better decision than your competitor every day.

Ponder this:

Decisions have the power to move everyone around you forward in a faster way, and that can be a competitive advantage for you and your team.

WHERE AND WHY

Many rush to the HOW and WHEN
before determining the WHERE AND WHY.

Ponder this:

*A very clear WHERE and WHY will give you more
emotional energy to do the HOW and WHEN.
Invest time to get clear on the WHERE and WHY.*

CUSTOMER EXPERIENCE

Successful businesses emphasize the customer experience in their value proposition.

Ponder this:

You make the biggest difference to your customers when you first focus on the experience you are creating for them before your products / services.

KNOW WITHOUT THE NO

A big danger of knowledge is thinking that you know what's impossible.

Ponder this:

Knowledge has a way of closing down routes to achieving the impossible. Use your knowledge to fuel insights and ideas, rather than saying "No" to the impossible.

DECIDE, COMMIT, EXECUTE

Business is about doing 3 things well:
Decisions, Commitment and Execution

Ponder this:

Direction is set by your decisions. Commitment is set by your actions. Execution is set by how you ensure that the right actions are being taken.

ADVICE WITH YOUR OWN JUDGMENT

Get great at balancing the advice from others and your own business judgment.

Ponder this:

Invest the time to listen to others, and always use their advice to evaluate your own business judgment. Never blindly follow other people's advice.

DO AN INVESTMENT REVIEW

Start with yourself, as your own personal growth pays the highest return.

Ponder this:

An investment review is key at the onset.
You are your most important investment.
Are you investing enough in you?

COMPETITION WITH YOURSELF

The strongest competitors compete with themselves to achieve their full potential.

Ponder this:

The strongest competitors focus on their biggest competitor...their own potential. It's a competitor that will never ever surrender.

DRIVEN/COMPETITIVE

Compete with others and your focus falls on others rather than on doing your best.

Ponder this:

Competing can be limiting, as it takes the focus off yourself. Keep the focus on you, and on what you can do to become better each day.

DISADVANTAGE TO ADVANTAGE

A little fresh thinking can turn a
disadvantage into an advantage.

Ponder this:

*A disadvantage will remain a disadvantage
unless you invest some time to explore ideas that
might reduce or eliminate the disadvantage.*

WAIT FOR OR CREATING IT

The unsuccessful wait for their future, while the successful start creating it.

Ponder this:

Don't wait for others to provide you with opportunity. Focus your own action and somehow the opportunities will always find you.

LEARN, USE AND ACHIEVE

Some learn, but don't use. Some use but, don't achieve. Successfully learn, use and achieve!

Ponder this:

It's not what you learn that makes you a success.
It is what you learn and then use.

CONFIDENCE TO ADAPT

Success in complex organizations is driven by our ability to adapt.

Ponder this:

Unless you have energy, you will never attract people with energy around you. Focus on keeping your mindset positive and show your energy to others.

AUTHENTIC ENERGY IS CONTAGIOUS

Show your energy and attract the
energy of those around you too.

Ponder this:

*Energy is a magnet. When you show your energy,
you attract the energy of everyone around you too.
How energetic do you feel today?*

EVERY BUSINESS IS A PEOPLE BUSINESS

For successful leaders, business success always starts with the people.

Ponder this:

Your people are your most important asset.
Value your people pipeline. Keep growing every level
so you will have competent replacements.

REQUIRES A CULTURE CHANGE

Company turnarounds are enabled by a leadership led culture change.

Ponder this:

A turnaround in performance is enabled by a turnaround in the culture. Focus your leadership on both the performance and culture change.

STRONG COMPETITOR

Great competitors start with themselves, and compete with their own potential.

Ponder this:

Competition is fierce and getting fiercer.
The only way to stay ahead of it is to continually invest in
your self-development and chasing your potential.

EVEN IF VERSUS IF

Achieve success with an EVEN IF mindset, and make it happen no matter what.

Ponder this:

Grow your EVEN IF mindset and you will find a way to achieve no matter what circumstances or obstacles stand in your way.

CREATE A DROP LIST

Find more time for the important by stopping what's unimportant.

Ponder this:

You can be more productive by identifying what you shouldn't be doing. No one ever gets to the bottom of their wish list every day.

ONE THING AT A TIME

Grow by focusing on a single improvement, then make it a permanent habit.

Ponder this:

Focus on one personal improvement at a time. Pick the right habit. It may have an impact on everything else.

YOU PERFORM AS YOU PREPARE

You can recognize champions by how they practice and prepare for competition.

Ponder this:

Notice how you do your preparation, as it will be a predictor of how you will perform. Prepare your best to perform at your best.

COMPETITION CAN BE LIMITING

Focusing on competition with others can limit your potential.

Ponder this:

If you focus on the competition, you put the focus on others. Focus on using your potential, and your focus drives you to become better every day.

HALFWAY IS NO WAY

Make the commitment at the beginning
to do whatever it takes to go all the way.

Ponder this:

*When you make the commitment at the start,
you are then prepared to do whatever it takes to achieve it.
Start with your commitment.*

MORE WITH LESS

Within every business there's always a foundation: strive to do more with less.

Ponder this:

If you focus on doing more with less, you will find more ways to be more productive and just naturally keep your focus stronger as well.

IN THE SAME DIRECTION

All leaders drive action. Successful leaders drive actions in the same direction.

Ponder this:

Direction is one of the most important communication focuses for your people. Only aligned action has real power to drive your team forward.

FIND AND LISTEN

Find the right people and listen, and you see the way to accomplish anything.

Ponder this:

Success is a team sport. Invest the time to find and listen to the right people, and you will get the knowledge and motivation to achieve anything.

REPETITION, THE KEY TO SUCCESS

Competence comes from learning, improving and repeating what you are doing.

Ponder this:

You can never be good at anything by just doing it occasionally. You need to invest the time to repeat it enough so it becomes more automatic.

CREATE VERSUS COMPETE

Compete and you are a reactive follower. Create and you are a pro-active leader.

Ponder this:

If you focus on competing, you may limit your creativity. Focus on creating and be more pro-active than re-active.

RESULTS DRIVEN AND PEOPLE FOCUSED

Business success is only achieved by
the great work of your people.

Ponder this:

*Results and numbers are important, but it is the direction
and confidence you provide your people that enables them
to deliver those results.*

PEOPLE LOOSE WITHIN A FRAMEWORK

If you don't have a framework in place, you always need to be more controlling.

Ponder this:

Successful delegators have a frame to manage how they delegate and adjust the framework to the level where they can trust their people's business judgment.

STRATEGY WITHOUT LEADERSHIP

Strategy without leadership is like building blocks without form.

Ponder this:

A strategy becomes valuable only when it is implemented. Strong leadership delivers the right decisions to keep the strategy moving forward.

HIRE GREAT PEOPLE

Success in business is all about the people, so invest in hiring the best.

Ponder this:

The most important process in your business is the hiring process. Are you dedicated to investing the right focus and effort into this process for every hire?

REFLECTION DRIVES FORESIGHT

Study the past. Learn lessons to
help avoid repeating past mistakes.

Ponder this:

*Reflection lets you use the past in productive ways,
and can often inspire new insights to make the
future even better.*

FUEL FOR WINNING

Confident people take action, take more risks, and inspire others to do the same.

Ponder this:

Take more action to keep your confidence high, and encourage everyone around you to do the same. Confidence is the fuel for winning in every part of your life.

PAY ATTENTION TO THE RIGHT THINGS

It's not about the ability to focus;
but focusing on the right things.

Ponder this:

*First, set your focus on the important, and then find
the best ways to maintain that focus every day.
Focus enables achievement.*

MAKE BUSINESS PERSONAL

When the company mission becomes personal to your people, the magic happens.

Ponder this:

In every conversation with your people, look for ways to share and reinforce the company mission in a way that becomes more personal for them.

DISCIPLINE DRIVES CONSISTENCY

Ability is important, but discipline is what drives consistency in your performance.

Ponder this:

Ability is multiplied when you have the discipline to consistently use it. Ability is potential and discipline helps you release that potential.

SUCCESS ATTRACTS GREAT PEOPLE

Achieve success and you attract great
people to help create even more success.

Ponder this:

*Success creates its own momentum, as it has a
way of attracting other successful people because
they think they can learn something from you.*

OFF THE WALL AND INTO ACTION

Powerful values / principles are not slogans on walls, but in the minds and hearts of everyone.

Ponder this:

Your team's values are only powerful if your people are living them. How would you recognize that your people are living core values?

GENERATE ENTHUSIASM

Enthusiasm is contagious. It not only impacts co-workers, but customers too.

Ponder this:

Enthusiasm creates an energy in all your conversations, and invites others to engage with you in more meaningful ways.

LOOK FOR A BETTER WAY

An improvement mindset is part of every successful team looking for better results.

Ponder this:

You will not see a successful team that is not always looking for a better way, using a mindset of continuous improvement in everything it does.

CREATE THE RIGHT CONVERSATIONS

You see progress when you have the right conversations with the right people.

Ponder this:

Schedule your conversations with the right people first. Schedule everything else you need to do to follow.

PLAYING THE WRONG GAME WELL

Doing what you are good at, but not passionate about, is playing the wrong game.

Ponder this:

When your work is not within your passion, you just don't have the energy to get better at it. Focus on work within your passion to become your best.

MAKE SENSE OF WHAT HITS YOU

There is power in being able to evaluate each situation as quickly as you can.

Ponder this:

You are more in control of your circumstances when you quickly evaluate them as to what they mean to you and what you can do about them.

CHARACTER AND COMPETENCE

Long-term success has a foundation in both character and competence.

Ponder this:

Build competence within your team and its members will find more opportunities.

HAVE A WINNING SPIRIT

Winners possess the spirit of winning, which is contagious!

Ponder this:

Recognize and reward even the small wins that your team and you achieve. This builds the spirit of winning in everyone.

PLAN A ENABLES A FASTER PLAN B

Planning is what enables you to adapt
quickly and develop a "Plan B," "Plan C," etc.

Ponder this:

*Planning ahead forces you to develop alternatives
that make you more ready for anything that could happen.
"Plan B" means being ready!*

FOREVER DOESN'T EXIST

You best processes don't live forever.
Continually evaluate what needs to change.

Ponder this:

*Evaluate your current processes, then invest the
time to change the processes that are no longer working
and are slowing you and your team down.*

WALK AND TALK THE VALUES

Values are only powerful when the leaders both walk and talk them every day.

Ponder this:

The chief values officer is you, and your own behavior is key to making your values powerful throughout your organization.

LEARN FROM YOUR MISTAKES

The worst mistake is the one you make
and fail to learn from.

Ponder this:

*Invest the time to learn from your mistakes, and use
the lessons learned to move forward faster.*

CHANGE YOUR LEVEL OF THINKING

You cannot take on a bigger challenge with the same thinking you have today.

Ponder this:

Big challenges require us to up our level of thinking in order to develop solutions that can address them. Make the investment in the time to THINK.

INTEGRATE ENCOURAGE AND PUSH

Leadership requires you to both encourage and push your team along the way.

Ponder this:

Treat everyone as an individual. Look for the best ways to both encourage and push all the people in the team to achieve their full potential.

COLLECTION 4

**Thoughts on Facing
a Big Challenge**

ONLY YOU SET THE LIMIT

Everyone has unlimited potential inside. Only you can decide what your limit is!

Ponder this:

Only you have the power to decide your potential. Never surrender that power to others or let them set your limits for you.

PREPARED TO GIVE YOUR BEST

People who give their best invest in the preparation required to make it happen.

Ponder this:

The best doesn't come without preparation.
Schedule your preparation time in first before fitting
everything else into your schedule after.

AVOID THE OBSTACLES

Get advice from experts to *avoid* obstacles rather than running into them.

Ponder this:

Why would you want to experience obstacles you can avoid? Invest time to get advice as early as possible at the start of any new initiative.

BEING YOURSELF AT YOUR BEST

Success comes slower when you try to be someone else. Be yourself and be your best.

Ponder this:

Don't try to be someone else. Take what they do and make it you own. You will make the biggest difference when you are YOU AT YOUR BEST.

FUEL FOR EXECUTION

A powerful vision creates the fuel to do whatever it takes to achieve it.

Ponder this:

Successful people start by knowing their own vision before they engage others in what they want to achieve. A clear vision can take on any challenge.

KEEP THE RESPONSIBILITY

Don't look for others to motivate you.
Accept that motivation is your own responsibility.

Ponder this:

*You will move too slowly if you wait for others
to motivate you. Learn what motivates you and make
it part of your daily life — a HABIT.*

HOW YOU SEE YOURSELF

More than other factors, how you see yourself determines what you achieve.

Ponder this:

Self-esteem can be one of the most important factors to your success, so what are you doing to both grow and maintain your self-esteem?

COMFORTABLE TO BE UNCOMFORTABLE

Faster growth comes by being comfortable continually taking on new challenges.

Ponder this:

Be strong enough to do the uncomfortable too. It enables you to take on challenges that help you achieve what you want far faster than you may have thought possible.

FAITH OVER FEAR

Fear / faith come from an unknown.
Conquer fear with faith.

Ponder this:

You reduce the impact of your fears by focusing on the faith that you can effectively deal with whatever happens to you.

PLANS CAN REDUCE MISTAKES

Investing in planning helps avoid mistakes made by overlooking the obvious.

Ponder this:

When you invest in planning ahead, you think it through so you don't miss the obvious and slow down your implementation.

FOUNDATION FOR GROWTH

A strong foundation supports a tall building.
Your strengths support a tall you.

Ponder this:

*Keep your focus on building upon your strengths.
Use them as a foundation for the growth you can achieve,
and the potential inside you.*

STEP THROUGH THE DOOR THAT OPENS

When opportunities come, don't say "I'm not ready." Instead, say "Let's go!"

Ponder this:

Be prepared and confident to take on opportunities when they arrive. Very often, timing is the most important part of taking advantage of an opportunity.

LET GO TO GROW

You can't take on new challenges without letting go of ones you can delegate.

Ponder this:

Unless you delegate more to your people, you are limiting the impact you can make. Some challenges will be left untouched.

ROAD TO SOMEWHERE

Where is your thinking taking you?
Forward or backward?

Ponder this:

*You become what you think about. Invest more time
in thinking about the future, because thinking of the past
only makes you more of what you once were,
rather than what you can be.*

PRECEDED BY A NEW BELIEF

To create more breakthroughs,
you have to believe in new possibilities.

Ponder this:

*Making more breakthroughs is often about
questioning old beliefs. Open your thinking to new ideas
you could not see before.*

WHAT YOU CHOOSE TO IGNORE

Effectiveness is focusing on the important, and making a choice on what you will ignore.

Ponder this:

Start by choosing what you will ignore. That will make more room for the important. Then, don't let what you choose to ignore re-grab your attention.

CHALLENGES CREATE INNER STRENGTH

It's the challenges you embrace that help
you to develop inner strength faster.

Ponder this:

*You grow more inner strength by what you embrace,
especially challenges. Seek out more challenges in order
to build your inner strength faster.*

NEW OR REPEATED EXPERIENCES

Repetitive experiences foster a limiting mindset. New experiences expand it.

Ponder this:

Seek out new experiences every day and you will never have the problem of a limited mindset. It will just naturally keep growing.

WHAT AND WHY UNCOVERS THE HOW

Don't rush to the "how" before getting clarity on what it is you really want and why.

Ponder this:

Invest time to get clear on WHAT you want and WHY, and the HOW will become far more clear. Don't rush to the HOW without the right clarity.

THROUGH DIFFICULT CHOICES

Greater success is on the other side of difficult choices. Embrace tough decisions rather than avoid them.

Ponder this:

Choices are what drive your focus. Difficult choices are what often drive the value you can generate from your focus. So, embrace difficult choices.

IF YOU KNEW YOU COULD NOT FAIL

Stay determined to work as hard and as long as it takes to achieve success.

Ponder this:

The belief that you can do it will enable the discipline and determination you need to succeed... because you know you will.

TO BE GREAT, BE WITH GREAT PEOPLE

Focus on associating yourself with people you would like to be like.

Ponder this:

Find the right role models and look for ways to spend more time with them. To become great faster, copy the habits of the great.

REFLECTION LEADS TO INNOVATION

Invest in reflection time, as it is the time
when breakthroughs often start.

Ponder this:

*With dedicated thought, more insights and ideas
just naturally flow into your mind, helping you see
breakthroughs you couldn't see before.*

GIVE YOUR DREAMS A DATE

You never get a sense of urgency unless you put a date to your dreams.

Ponder this:

Dreams are important, but they must also have a date. Without a deadline, you will never create the sense of urgency in yourself to take daily action.

NOT AFRAID TO ASK THE QUESTION

What slows you down is the question
you are afraid to ask yourself.

Ponder this:

*Unasked questions slow your progress — and it is often the
questions you are afraid to ask that slow you down the
most. Ask yourself that scary question today!*

DETOX YOUR THINKING

A detox is about clearing the mind and focusing on what really matters.

Ponder this:

Invest in reflection time, so you can eliminate trivial thoughts that retard your progress toward what really matters.

ANXIETY IS FEAR BEING EXPRESSED

Anxiety is often coming from a fear
you have not faced.

Ponder this:

*You gain more power over your fears when you
have embraced them, thought them through,
and realized they cannot stop you.*

OFF YOUR PLATE

Trivia you take off your plate makes more room for important things.

Ponder this:

Understand what you shouldn't be doing, so you can stop it and make room for more time and effort on the truly important.

BIGGEST RISK IS NOT TAKING ACTION

The biggest risk in life is to not take action.
Without action you never use your full potential.

Ponder this:

*There are far more risks in not taking action than
in taking action. With every action you take, you are
using more of the potential you have inside you.*

DISCIPLINE TO REMAIN CALM

Invest time to build the right level of discipline to remain calm in difficult situations.

Ponder this:

Remaining calm comes from self-awareness and the discipline to maintain your composure in difficult situations. Invest in making self-discipline your habit.

EMBRACE WHAT YOU ARE RESISTING

Facing what you fear could open doors
to everything you want.

Ponder this:

*What you fear and resist could be the very thing
that holds you back. Embrace what you resist and
decide what you will do right now.*

WITH PURPOSE YOU GO BEYOND BELIEF

The real power of your ideas lies with the purpose that grew those ideas within you.

Ponder this:

The real power of your ideas is the WHY behind them. You get people going beyond understanding to believing when you add the WHY.

EMBRACE THE PRESSURE

Pressure is a call for action that always helps you grow faster.

Ponder this:

Pressure is a way of helping you to take more action. The more action you take, the more you learn and grow.

BACKUP PLANS REDUCE STRESS

Having a backup plan gives you the emotional strength to take more risks.

Ponder this:

Invest the time to think through your backup plan, and it will give you the confidence to take more risks on your main plan.

MORE TIME ON FEWER THINGS

Success is about dedicating more of your time to fewer things.

Ponder this:

If you don't prioritize, you end up doing more work for other people's priorities than your own. Define what is most important to you first.

KEEP IT ON THE FRONT BURNER

Whatever your make a priority guides your daily actions.

Ponder this:

Invest time to create and maintain clear priorities, as they provide the focus of what you do each day.

MILESTONES DRIVE SPEED

Milestones improve the speed of an initiative by keeping everyone on pace.

Ponder this:

Ask your people for the key milestones visible to everyone, as they will keep your people focused on both achievement and pace.

GROW MORE COGNITIVE SPACE

You make better decisions when you block off time to really think them through.

Ponder this:

You may say "I don't have time to think!" Block off time for reflection first, and you will make better decisions more often.

START THE WAY YOU WILL CONTINUE

Why not start fast and then focus on keeping up the pace? You will achieve results faster.

Ponder this:

The speed at the start of an initiative establishes a pace that tends to last. Drive yourself to start fast and to keep that pace until you achieve what you want.

DETERMINE IT TO PREPARE FOR IT

Determine up front what could happen.
Then you are better prepared for it.

Ponder this:

*Invest a little time to think through what could happen,
and you will be better prepared if you need to take action.*

SET ASIDE TIME FOR IT

Unless you set aside time for it,
you can't say it is a priority for you.

Ponder this:

*A great way to see if you have the right focus on
your priorities is to take notice of what you set time aside
for each day. Your time should be reserved for the
important rather than the trivial.*

USUALLY PLAYS OUT IN SMALL STEPS

A big vision usually plays out in small steps at the start — until you get momentum.

Ponder this:

Discipline yourself to keep taking those small steps. Suddenly the momentum will build and attract the help of others to take bigger steps.

YOUR BIGGEST SOURCE OF ERROR

Doubt drives you to make more mistakes as you don't put your full effort into a clear goal.

Ponder this:

Understand when doubt is the only thing holding you back, because it is stealing your potential in a very subtle way.

IT'S ALL GOOD NEWS

Take a positive view on everything
and it will fuel more momentum.

Ponder this:

*Look at the positive in every situation, and you will
see more action you can take. A positive attitude builds
momentum, while a negative outlook retards it.*

AWARENESS IS EVERYTHING

Unless you have awareness, you are taking action on false assumptions.

Ponder this:

Become more aware of yourself and the world around you, and you will make better assumptions in every initiative you undertake.

FACE FEARS TO GROW COURAGE

You can develop courage by facing
all the fears you visualize.

Ponder this:

*Face your fears rather than avoid them, and decide
right away what you will do to fully address them.*

SEEING YOUR CHOICES CLEARLY

You make better decisions when you clearly see the choices you have available.

Ponder this:

Focus first on clearly seeing the choices you have, and you will then feel more confident in making a decision.

EACH DAY IS THE KEY

To achieve any goal, it is what you do each day that enables you to achieve it.

Ponder this:

Focus on what you can do each day, and you can achieve any goal faster. So, what can you do today for your most important goal?

EXPERIENCE CAN CREATE BLIND SPOTS

Relying on only your own experience
sometimes limits where you find solutions.

Ponder this:

*Reach out for the help of others. Often the limits
of your own experience can blind you to solutions
coming from other places.*

WHAT YOU CARRY ALONG WITH YOU

Your thoughts are either lightening
your load or making it heavier.

Ponder this:

*Be aware of your thoughts, as they either help
you to achieve more or slow you down. Keep your
thoughts positive and strong.*

THROUGH THE DISCOMFORT PERIOD

Within every change, there is a discomfort period before you embrace the new.

Ponder this:

Success often comes from your ability to drive yourself through uncomfortable times until progress refuels your desire to achieve it.

BELIEF IS WHAT MATTERS

If you don't believe, everything you do
will be much harder.

Ponder this:

*Check your beliefs first. Your belief in what you
are trying to accomplish is helping you...and can make
the biggest difference to your success.*

COLLECTION 5

Thoughts on Helping Others Achieve Their Goals

HAPPY FOR WHO?

Are you happy when you help others
or happy for the people you help?

Ponder this:

*When you help others, you are not only making them
happy, but yourself too. You get the same feeling of
achievement when you help others achieve.*

LIFTING OTHERS LIFTS YOU

You lift your own spirits
when you help others.

Ponder this:

*You lift your own spirits by acting as a role model for
others. By being the best you for the sake of others, you
become the best you for yourself.*

BRING OUT THEIR BEST QUALITIES

Build a strong rapport with others,
and you bring out their best qualities.

Ponder this:

You get the best from others when you develop a great rapport with them. Rapport encourages others to listen more closely to what you say and what you ask.

YOU CHANGE FROM WITHIN

You cannot change others; you can only help them
see the potential for change within themselves.

Ponder this:

*Focus on getting others thinking, feeling and talking.
You cannot change others, but you can help them see the
possibilities for growth within themselves.*

ENOUGH TO SEE THE ACTION

Your people need clarity in order to direct their actions without your help.

Ponder this:

Always keep testing and reinforcing the clarity of your people so that they can take more action without always checking with you.

HELP THEM BUILD THEIR BRAND

Help your people build their own personal brand to better support their careers.

Ponder this:

Your people appreciate it when you help them better understand themselves and learn how to package their strengths in more valuable ways.

SUPPORT THE IDEAS OF YOUR PEOPLE

Words of support will turn your people's ideas into action and achievement.

Ponder this:

Your people will take more action and more risks when they feel they have total support for their ideas from their leader.

INVEST IN PEOPLE WHO INVEST

The worst investment is helping someone
who is unwilling to help themselves.

Ponder this:

*Hire people who are focused on their own
self-development. This makes your time developing
them a worthwhile investment.*

ACCOUNTABILITY ATTRACTS

Those who feel accountable for their actions get more help from others too.

Ponder this:

People around you will feel good about helping you when they see you honoring your commitments first. Action from you promotes action from others.

RELATIONSHIP TO THE TEAM

Define team success as an "AND." It's about both individual AND team success.

Ponder this:

Team success is about leveraging everyone's individual success and orchestrating conversations that foster better collaboration across the team.

SEE FOR THEMSELVES

Teaching others is effective when they can see the lesson for themselves.

Ponder this:

Success in teaching others is not about you, but about them. Focus on helping others learn for themselves.

BELIEF IN THEIR ABILITY

The successful are constantly helping others believe in their abilities.

Ponder this:

You are only as powerful as the people around you, so constantly build the belief in those around you in achieving more together.

SHOW THEM WHAT THEY CAN DO

Delegating difficult challenges to others helps them see what they really can do.

Ponder this:

Unless you delegate the difficult, you are limiting your people and not using their abilities to the fullest. Don't be afraid to delegate the difficult.

HELP THEM ACHIEVE IT

Focus on helping your people achieve goals versus telling them what to do.

Ponder this:

Help your people achieve what you want without telling them how to do it. Telling is stopping your people from growing.

TRUST ENCOURAGES CREATIVITY

When your people feel you trust them, they look at more creative solutions.

Ponder this:

Trust enables your people to take more risks, often seeing solutions that would have otherwise been overlooked.

SEE THE WAY TO START

People struggle to get started, so leaders need to help their people see a way to start.

Ponder this:

The first step in any initiative is often the hardest one, so invest time with your people to help them see the fastest way to begin.

CAPTURE THE EXACT WORDS

People respond better when you use
their way of saying things.

Ponder this:

*Write down the exact words of important things others say
and then use their way of saying it in all of your follow-up
communications.*

DEVELOP THE MEANING FOR OTHERS

Communications have power when they helps others to develop their own meaning.

Ponder this:

Your communications are more powerful when you get your people to uncover their own meaning from the conversation, not just understand yours.

LEAD BY EXAMPLE

Leaders have a larger influence on others by their actions than their words.

Ponder this:

You are a role model, and others tend to copy your behaviors. Be the best you can be as your behaviors have more impact than your words.

REWARD PEOPLE FOR SMALL STEPS TOO

Recognize small steps and you encourage your team to make constant progress.

Ponder this:

*Recognize the importance of small steps,
as they provide steady encouragement to make
progress toward larger achievements.*

HELP PEOPLE KNOW WHAT'S POSSIBLE

Sometimes your people need extra encouragement to "try" the possible.

Ponder this:

Let your people know it's fine to try and fail a few times. Mitigating their fear of failure allows them to challenge themselves when an outcome is not a sure thing.

HELP MORE, JUDGE LESS

When you catch yourself judging others, ask "How can I help them?"

Ponder this:

Judging doesn't move things forward. Instead of judging others, look for ways that you can help them improve.

EXCITING PEOPLE AROUND AN IDEA

Getting people excited about their goals helps everyone make it happen faster.

Ponder this:

Helping your people understand the goals is not enough. You need to get them excited so that they will look for more creative ways to achieve them.

MAKE IT THEIR ANSWER

Encourage and facilitate your people
to find their own solutions.

Ponder this:

*Your people often know what to do and can find their
own solutions. Invest more time to encourage them to
use what they already know.*

DEMANDING, BUT WITH FLEXIBILITY

Understanding how to push and motivate each person is a key skill of leadership.

Ponder this:

Leadership is successful at the personal level.
You need to engage each person in a different way and
use a different mix of push and pull to drive them.

HELP OTHERS HELP THEMSELVES

The best gift you can ever give is helping others see how to help themselves.

Ponder this:

Don't be so fast to provide the easy answer to others. Let them learn how to find answers for themselves, and they grow stronger.

CLEAR VISION HAS PULLING POWER

When people have a clear direction,
it pulls them toward their goals.

Ponder this:

*Focus on creating and maintaining a clear direction.
This will create energy within people to pull them
toward success.*

OUT OF THEIR COMFORT ZONES

Challenges stretch your people out of their comfort zones and help them grow.

Ponder this:

The best leaders focus on creating challenges in incremental steps so their people keep growing – and build the confidence to grow even more.

CHALLENGE IDEAS NOT PEOPLE

Challenge the idea, not the person, and help your people think through the issue.

Ponder this:

It doesn't have to get personal. Challenge people's ideas in such a way that you don't make it personal. Keep it about the idea and not the person.

RESPECT DIFFERENCES

Respect the differences of others,
and you will be less frustrated.

Ponder this:

*Differences can contribute to solutions and help us
grow faster. When you respect that others can be different
from you, you don't get frustrated by them.*

GIVE CLEAR FEEDBACK

Clear feedback helps your people to take action faster and improve faster.

Ponder this:

Be strong enough to provide clear feedback, and your people will grow faster, becoming more valuable to you and your organization.

LIGHTING THE PATH FOR OTHERS

Light the path for your people to guide
their daily actions.

Ponder this:

*If the direction is clear in your people, they can define
their own way to get there. Communicate and reinforce
the direction in different ways each day.*

FEAR REDIRECTED CREATES ENERGY

The successful redirect their fear from avoidance to acceptance, embracing it and taking action.

Ponder this:

Avoiding fears reduces energy. Embracing fears allows people to identify the action they can take. It also creates more energy in them to take that action.

KNOW WHEN TO BACK OFF

Have the emotional intelligence to understand how far you can push people.

Ponder this:

Your people don't always want to do what's good for them. Listen and be open to adapting what you ask of them.

FREEDOM TO TAKE RISKS

Your people need the space to think for themselves and take their own risks.

Ponder this:

Encourage your people to think for themselves and take risks. This is the only way to stretch the limits of both your people and your organization.

ADDRESS THEIR DOUBTS AND FEARS

Help your people with their doubts and fears, and you speed their progress.

Ponder this:

Your people's doubts and fears slow them down more than their competences. Instill confidence in your people to take action in spite of doubts.

GIVE HOPE TO OTHERS

Hope is an enabler of the right belief,
and the right belief inspires more action.

Ponder this:

Leaders are the providers of hope. It's the belief the team possesses that helps it achieve the goal.

CREATE A CULTURE OF SHARING

When your people share more, they are enabling each other to deliver more too.

Ponder this:

Create ways for your people to share ideas and help each other, and you will be enabling them to achieve more.

POSITIVE PULL OR NEGATIVE PUSH

Negative push is fear, and doesn't last.
Positive pull is pride and lasts longer.

Ponder this:

Find ways to create more pride in your team, and you create a strong pull to achieve results. Pull (pride) is far more powerful than Push (fear).

INFLUENCE AND AUTHORITY

Influence and authority are not the same. Authority is more limited in its power.

Ponder this:

Focus on growing your influence with others, as your authority is limited by your role. Your influence has no formal limits.

TO IMPROVE PERFORMANCE - GO HOME

If you are always there to provide the easy answer, others will never learn to find solutions on their own.

Ponder this:

If your people come with a problem, insist that they also propose some solutions. Giving answers alone discourages your people from thinking independently.

GUIDE THE CONVERSATIONS

One role of a leader is to guide conversations so your people own the discussion.

Ponder this:

Ask more questions in your conversations.
When you do, your people feel they have been heard more,
and they will feel more confident to achieve what
they commit to.

EMPOWER - ENABLE MORE POWER

Empowerment is a buzzword,
but so powerful.

Ponder this:

*When you delegate decisions and give more
power to your people, you gain more power yourself.*

BRING EVERYONE UP A LEVEL

Raise your people's level of thinking
and you raise their actions too.

Ponder this:

*Focus on asking questions that get your people thinking
at higher levels about a situation, and they will better
understand the impact of their actions too.*

STAKE IN THE OUTCOME

People take ownership of their actions when they have a stake in the outcome.

Ponder this:

Personally connect the actions of your people to the outcome, and they will take more ownership. They will also work better as a team to achieve it.

HELP OTHERS LIVE THEIR CALLING

Everyone has a unique talent, so help others use it in the best ways they can.

Ponder this:

Help your people use their special talents (their "sweet spots") as this gives them more energy for what they do.

CREATE A NEW UNDERSTANDING

A big influence starts by helping others with a new understanding of the situation.

Ponder this:

You influence others when you get them to think about a situation in a new way. Ask more questions to expand the thinking and understanding of others.

WHO DESERVE YOUR CONFIDENCE

Your people deserve your confidence to grow faster and deliver more.

Ponder this:

Show your people you have confidence in them, and they will take on more challenges, grow faster, and achieve more too.

BEGIN BY REDUCING THEIR FEARS

Fear is what slows people down,
so first focus on reducing their fears.

Ponder this:

*Fear, not a lack of competence, is what slows your
people down the most. Invest in building your people's
confidence to take action by facing their fears.*

HELP THEM TO VIEW IT DIFFERENTLY

To get different behaviors, help others
see the situation differently.

Ponder this:

*Your power leading others comes from your ability
to get your people to think, and to think differently.
It starts with the questions you ask.*

EXPAND VERSUS LIMIT INFLUENCE

Help your people expand their influence, don't micro manage and limit it.

Ponder this:

Delegate more decisions and give more power to your people. As you expand their influence, you are also expanding yours too. Stop micromanaging.

HELP OTHERS SEE AN ACTION

When people struggle, help them see an action they can take.

Ponder this:

Most problems come from a lack of action. When your people struggle, help them see the action they can take to improve.

ABOUT THE
DAILY THOUGHTS
FOUNDATION

The Daily Thoughts Foundation was founded in September 2005 to:

- *Make a Difference Forever*
- *Leave a Legacy*
- *Create a Powerful Self-Development Habit*
- *Help You Keep Growing*

These goals inspired Mark Fritz to write more than 18,000 thoughts, completed on 11th March, 2017: enough daily thoughts to last 50 years!

The engine behind the writing was a habit of consistent study. In 2005, Fritz developed a habit that continues today. "Back then," he says, "I invested 60 days to push myself to study (read a book, listen to books, interviews, podcasts, etc.) whenever I was outside the home and by myself. By doing it all the time for those 60 days, I was able to create a habit, wiring myself to always search for study materials whenever I am by myself and outside the home. This has enabled me to average 60 minutes of daily study since September 2005, some days less and some days a lot more — especially when I am traveling. Also, the goal of making a difference forever provided the emotional fuel to do the studying, and to write the daily thoughts inspired by what I learned each day.

"Now that the daily thoughts are completed, the next goal is to produce books that will share the daily thoughts within different collections and all profits from the sale of these books going to charities that develop tomorrow's international leaders. These collections will come in the form of printed books and ebooks."

You can sign up to become a member of the **Daily Thoughts Foundation** and receive an email each day with the day's thought at the **Daily Thoughts Foundation** website:

www.dailythoughtsfoundation.com

DAILY THOUGHTS
ON THE GO

Each of the five collections in the paperback *Daily Thoughts Collections, Volume I* by Mark Fritz includes 52 thoughts, carefully gleaned from more than 18,000 daily thoughts published online by the **Daily Thoughts Foundation.** They are available individually as remarkably affordable Kindle editions, portable to accompany you on your daily travels.

The five Kindle editions are:

Living a Fulfilling Life
Managing Your Time
Gaining a Competitive Edge
Facing a Big Challenge
Helping Others Achieve Their Goals

Each of these collections will inspire new thoughts within you and help you grow faster, take more action and achieve more in life. Preview or order at:

www.dailythoughtsfoundation.com/collections

32090741R00165

Printed in Great Britain
by Amazon